The Usborne
Big Maze Book

Designed and illustrated by
Ruth Russell
Nayera Everall and Candice Whatmore

Written by Kirsteen Robson

The mazes at the beginning of the book are easier
and they get more challenging as you go through.
You'll find solutions to all the mazes on pages 61-64.

Penguin playtime

Can you help Percy the penguin across the ice field to
join his playmates (without getting his flippers wet)?

Percy

Digger dilemma

Dougie needs to drive his digger to the patch marked X to dig a hole. Unfortunately the blue digger has been shifting the heavy rocks around and has made a mess. Which way should Dougie go?

Dougie's digger

Start here

DIG HERE ↓

Anthill antics

The ants are celebrating spring. Wes the worker ant needs to tell each friend with a leaf to follow him to the **Great Hole** to prepare for the feast. Which route should he take?

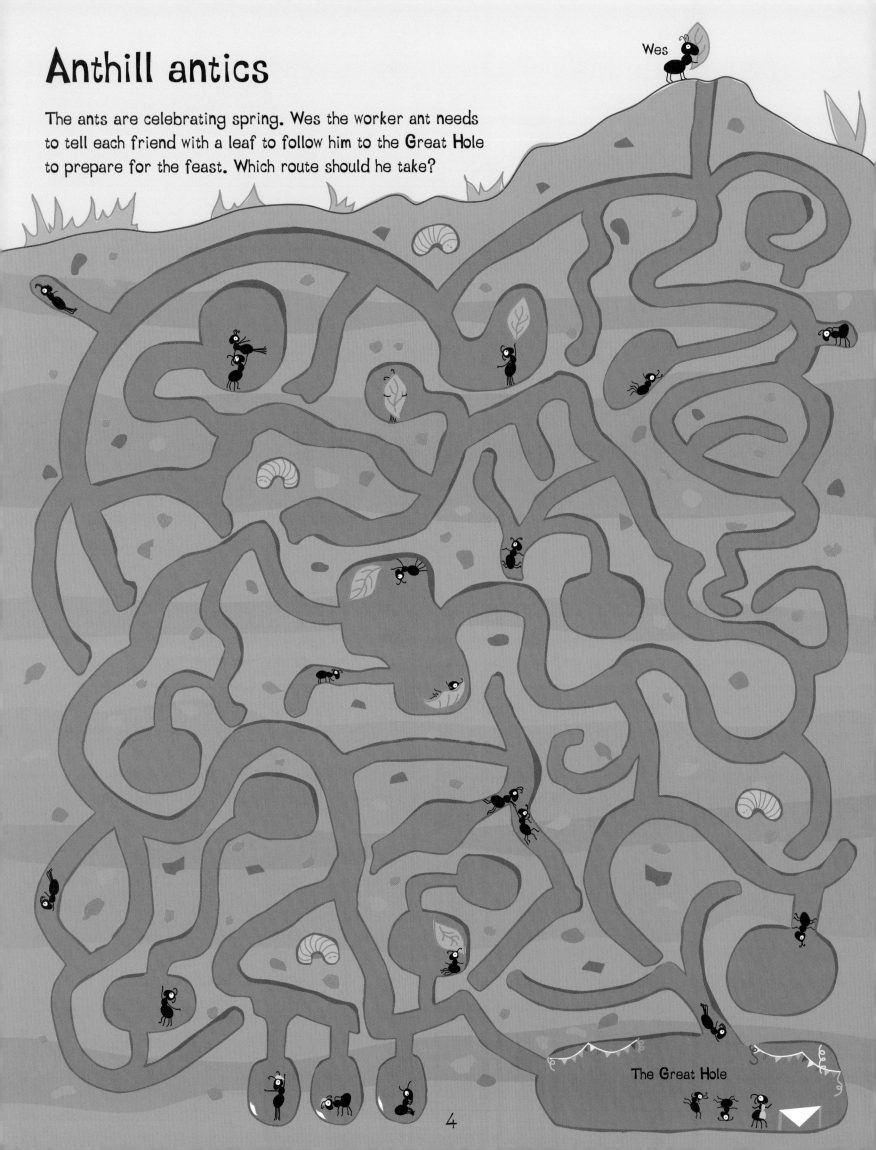

Wes

The Great Hole

Cloudy peril

Guide the plane safely between the clouds to the runway.

On safari

Can you plan a safari route to see wildebeests, elephants, giraffes, hippos, lions, leopards, flamingos, zebras, rhinos and crocodiles – in that order? You need to visit every hideout to get a really good view and you can't take the same track twice.

Hideouts look like this.

Start and finish here

The shelf run

How will the mouse get back to its hole? It can run along a shelf where there's nothing in its way. At the gaps, it can jump across between shelves or down to the shelf below.

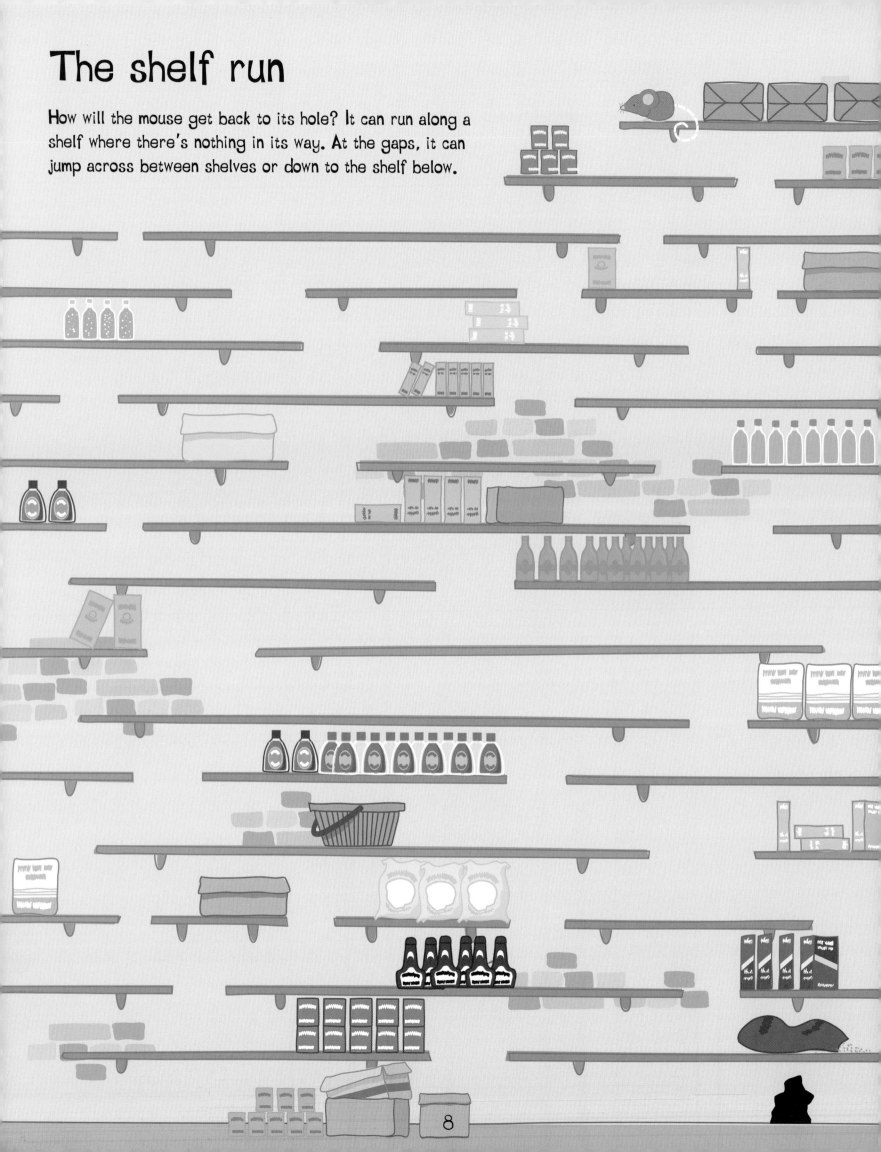

Hidden surprise

Can you help Harry find his surprise
birthday present? How many doorways
will he go through on the way?

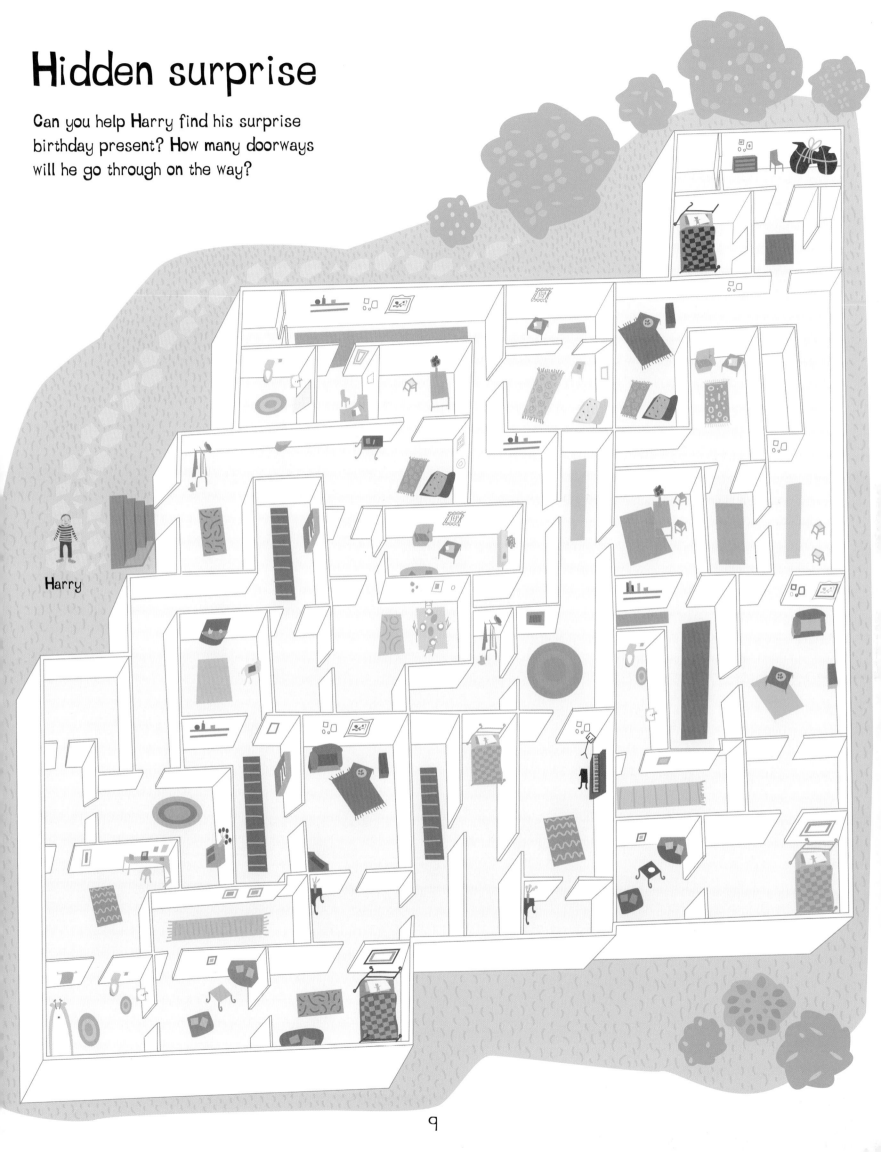

Harry

Traffic trouble

Can you find a way to cross the busy road? (Luckily, all the vehicles have stopped.)

Start here

Spiny starfish

Can you draw a path from the sandy shore to the water's edge without touching any starfish?

Start here

Farm visit

Take a trip around the farm, following the activity trail shown on the right. (You may cross a path you've taken, but you can't walk along the same path more than once.)

Start here

Farmhouse

ACTIVITY TRAIL

1. Pick some carrots from the vegetable patch and take them to the ponies in the field
2. Lead one of the ponies to the stable
3. Feed the pigs
4. Feed the sheep
5. Feed the ducks then play on the swings
6. Pick some apples as you walk around the orchard
7. Watch the cows being milked
8. Gather the eggs from the hens and take them to the farmhouse, taking time to stop and look at the wild flowers on the way

Dingle's Pond

Vegetable patch

Lower Meadow

Dingle Dell

The Pink Piggery

The Pony Paddock

Olga's Orchard

The Old Cow Shed

Green Pastures

The Twin Bridges

Sunny Lane Stables

Henhouses

Upper Meadow

Fresh Fields

Button match maze

Can you find your way through
the maze to another button
like this?

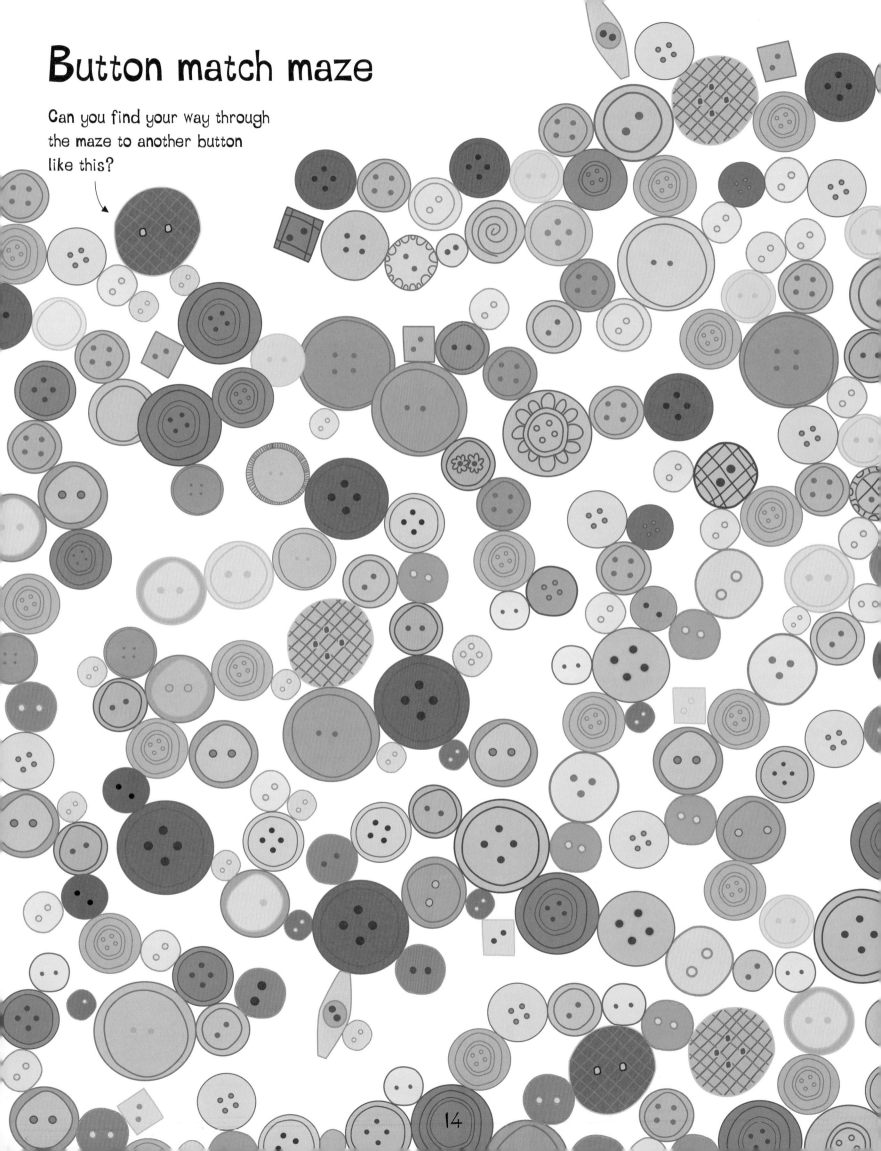

Campsite confusion

The twins have lost their way. They know they must stick to the campsite paths - but can you help them back to their tent? (Their tent is the only orange and yellow one on the site.)

Beware of the bears

Find a safe route for the salmon to swim to their breeding waters, avoiding any hungry bears and fearless fishermen that block their way. Waterfalls are not a problem - the salmon can jump up them.

Finish here

16

Start here

17

Lost fish

Help Goldie find her brother. She can swim through any gaps where the fish are **not** touching.

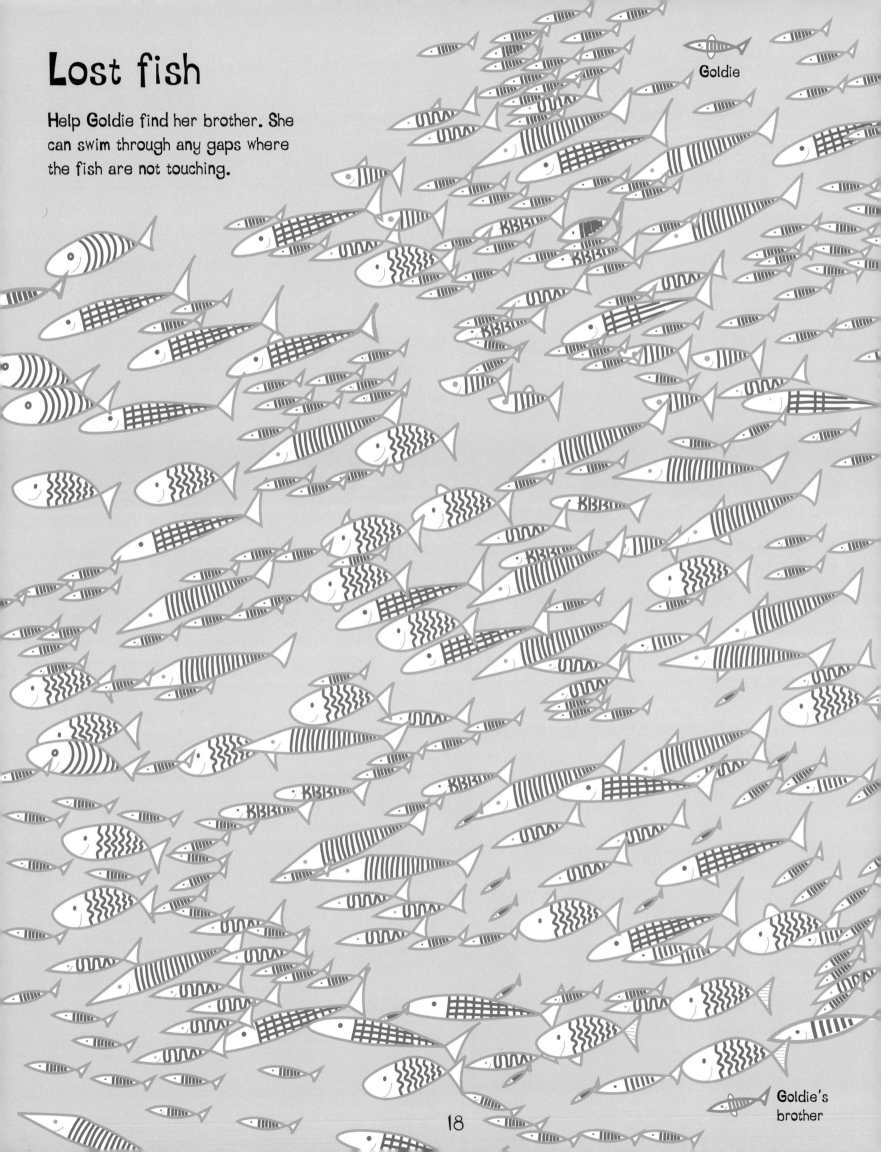

Goldie

Goldie's brother

Walking home

Sam always stops at the swings on the way home from school. Today she also needs to buy a loaf of bread, some flowers, and some toffees on the way back. What's the best route for her to take?

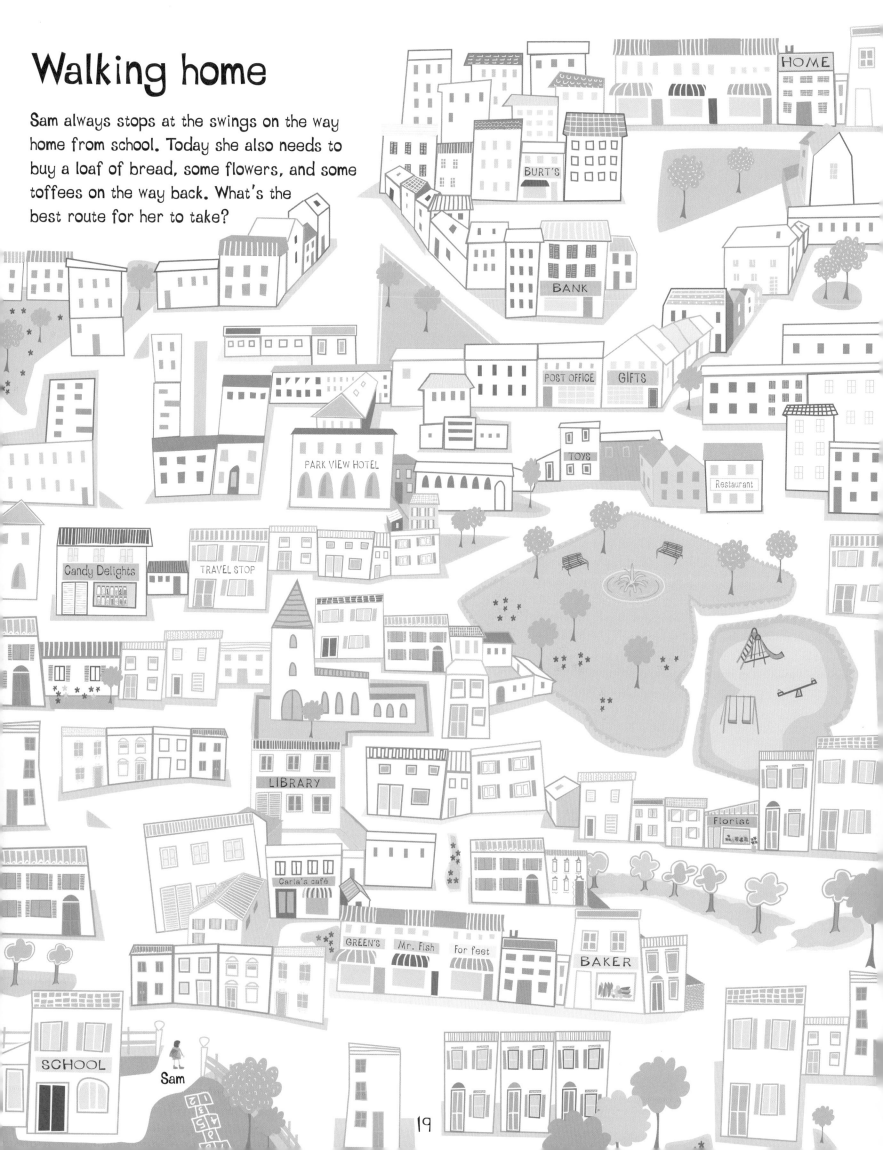

Sauce and sprinkles

Only one of the buttons on the ice cream sauce machine will work. But can you find out which one?

Feeding flamingos

Florence has spotted a space in the middle of the lake. Can you help her wade her way to it?

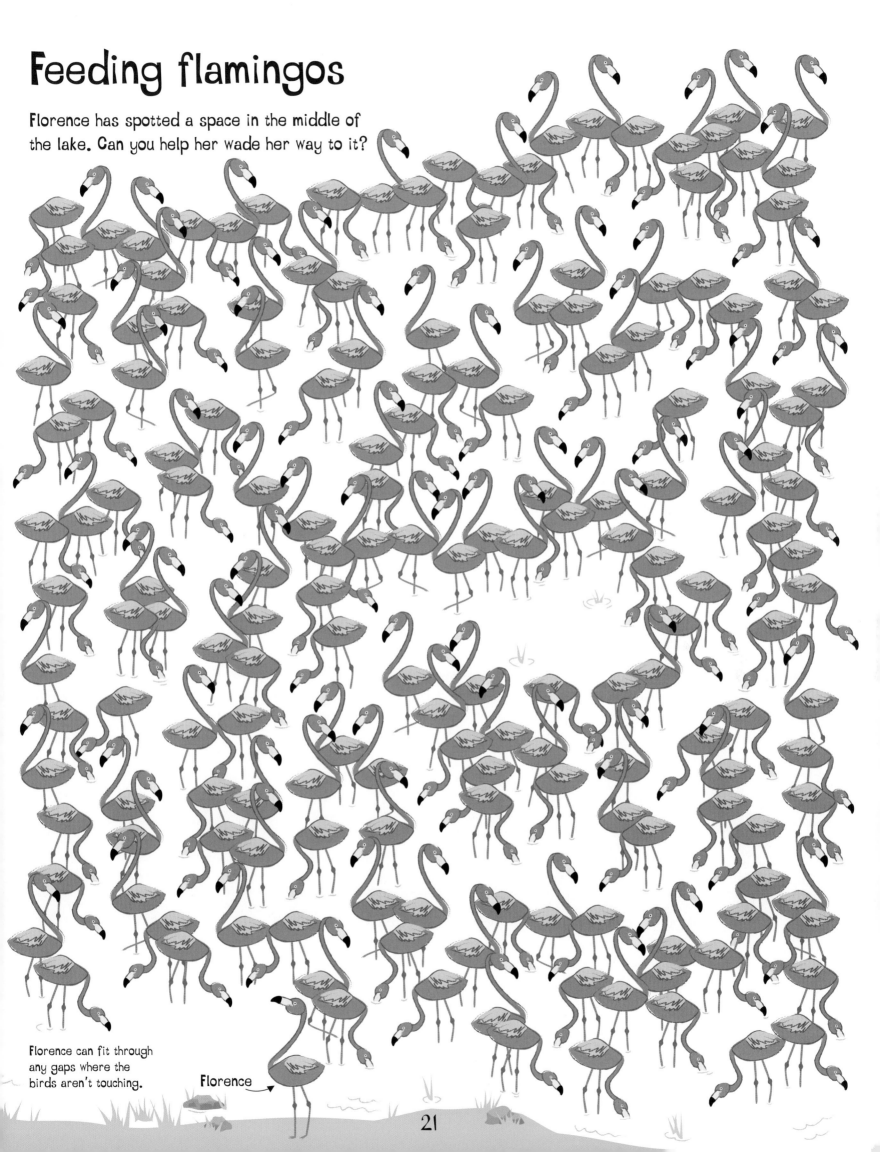

Florence can fit through
any gaps where the
birds aren't touching.

Florence →

21

Galaxy challenge

Can you help the flying saucer find its way across the galaxy to its home planet, avoiding the star fields and other space obstacles?

Start

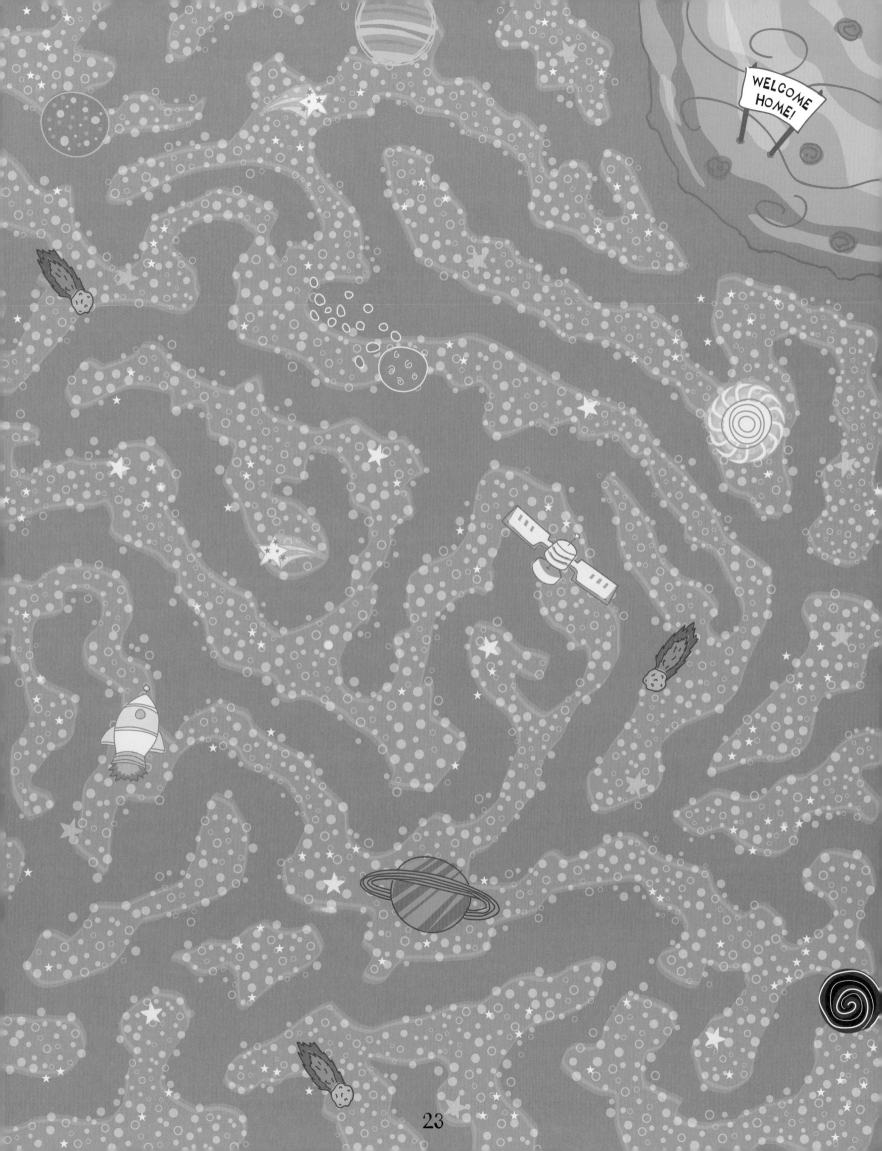

WELCOME HOME!

River rapids

Which way should the canoe go to pass safely through the swirling rapids and continue smoothly down the river?

Vegetable patch puzzle

Help Bobtail the bunny pick a path between the lettuces to the carrot patch. He needs to meet both his bunny friends on the way, but avoid the birds and gardening tools.

Bobtail

Daisy chain tangle

Show how this lonely little bug can squeeze through the spaces to meet its four spotted friends. It can fit through any gaps where the daisies are not touching.

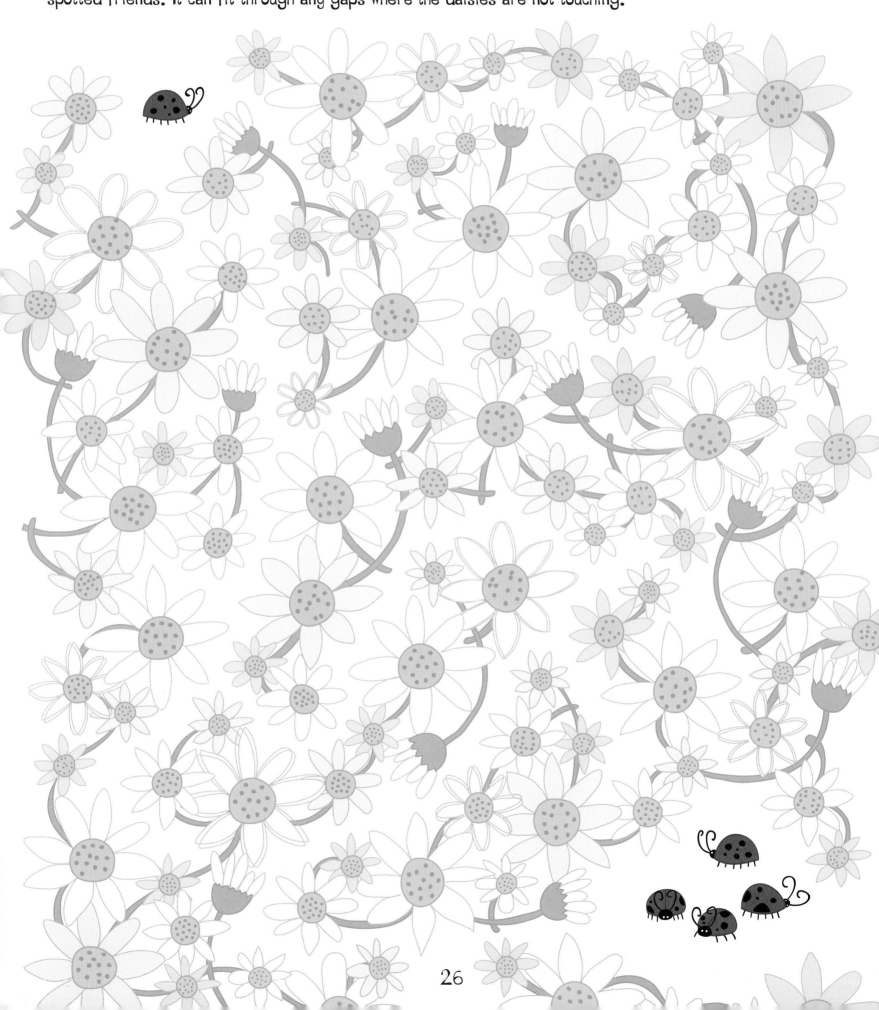

26

Jellyfish jumble

Help the orange octopus baby swim to its mother. It can squeeze through the spaces where the jellyfish don't touch.

Treasure Island

Find the shortest route for the ship to sail safely to the pirate treasure. It cannot sail past islands with skulls on them, and must avoid monster-infested lagoons at all costs.

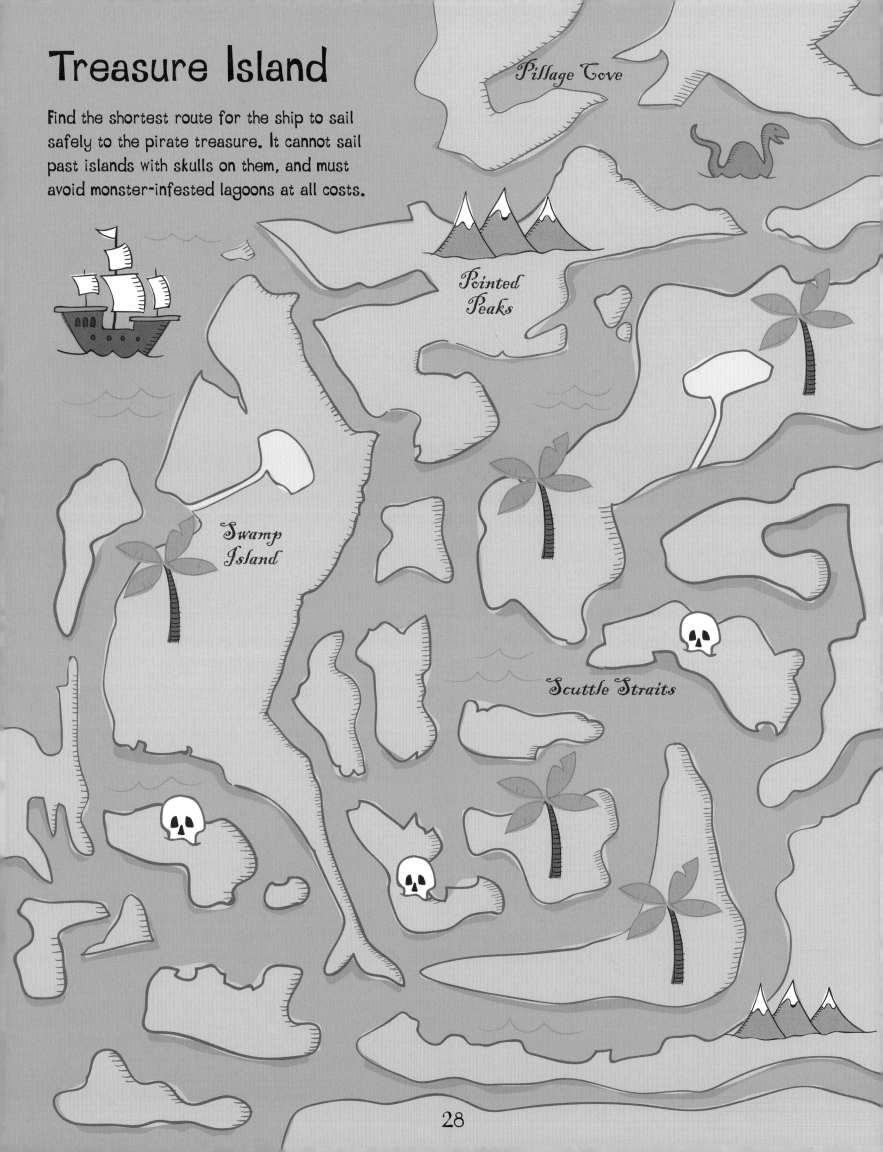

Pillage Cove

Pointed Peaks

Swamp Island

Scuttle Straits

Land of
No Hope

Buccaneer
Beach

Cutlass
Creek

Dead Man's
Island

Treasure
Island

Land of
No Hope

Chess mess

The chess championship is over and you need to put all the pieces away. But first see if you can lead this green bishop to the other one. You can move it across all four boards, but you are only allowed to move diagonally onto empty white squares.

Bishop

Start here

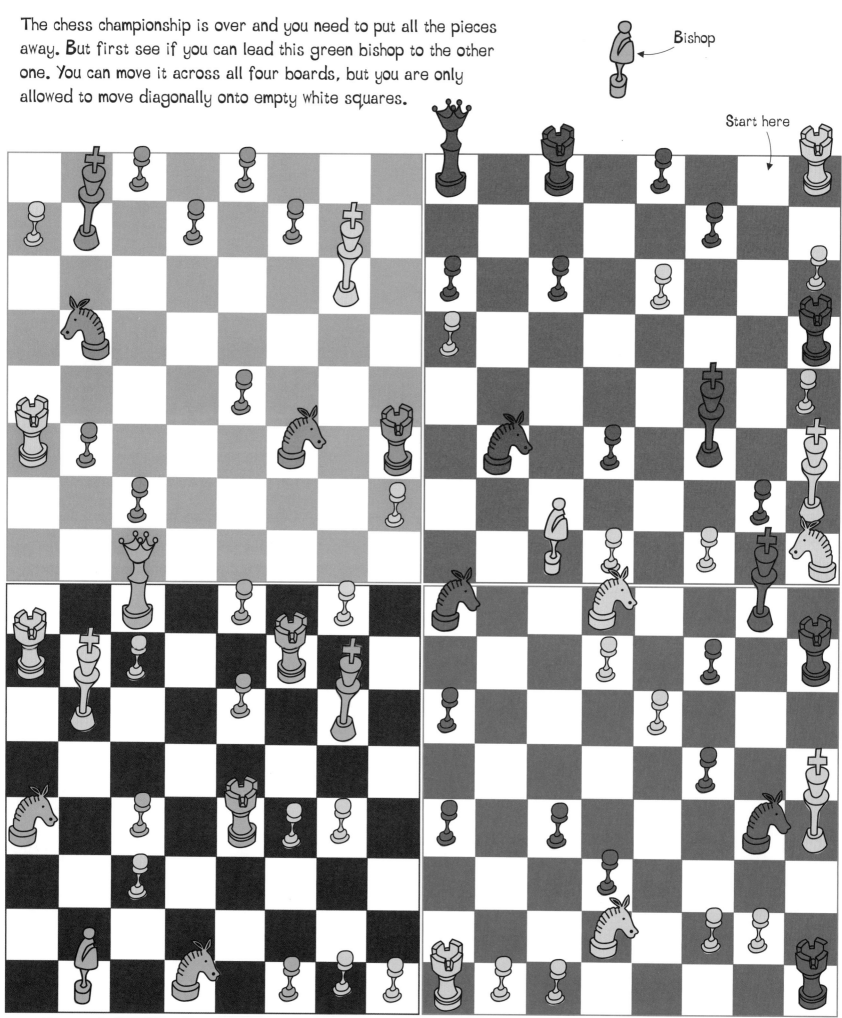

Puzzle planet

Can you help Zob the alien find the quickest
path across the planet back to his spaceship?

Zob

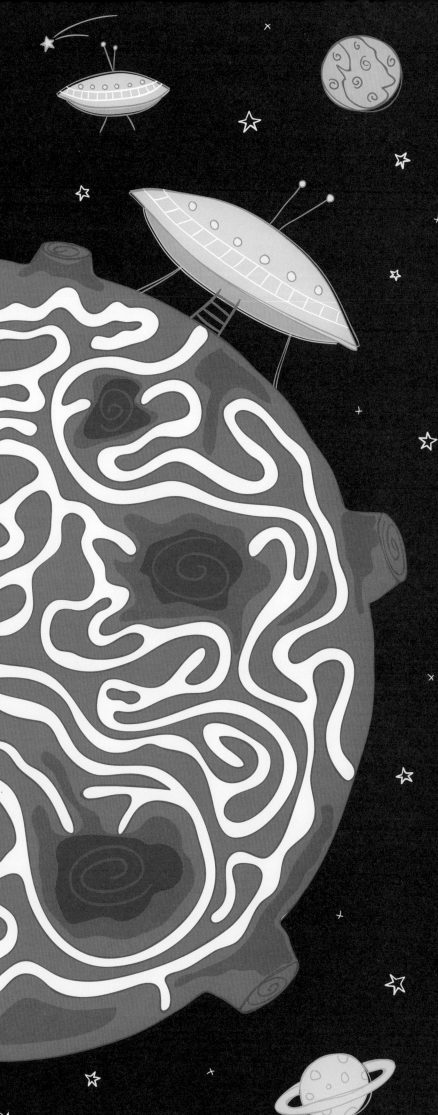

Santa's sleighride

Which swirly smoke trail will lead Santa to a chimney?

Start here

Birds and branches

Which is the shortest route for the baby bird to hop along the branches from the ground to the nest without meeting any other birds?

34

Start here

Pencil box muddle

The pink pen has lost its top. Draw a path with your pencil so you can reach the top without touching anything on the table.

Start here

Lily pad race

Two frogs are going to race to the crown sitting on the giant lily pad. Freddie thinks it's a shorter route across the lily pads, avoiding pale green leaves or leaves with holes in them. Fergus decides to swim between the lily pad paths. Who will win the royal prize?

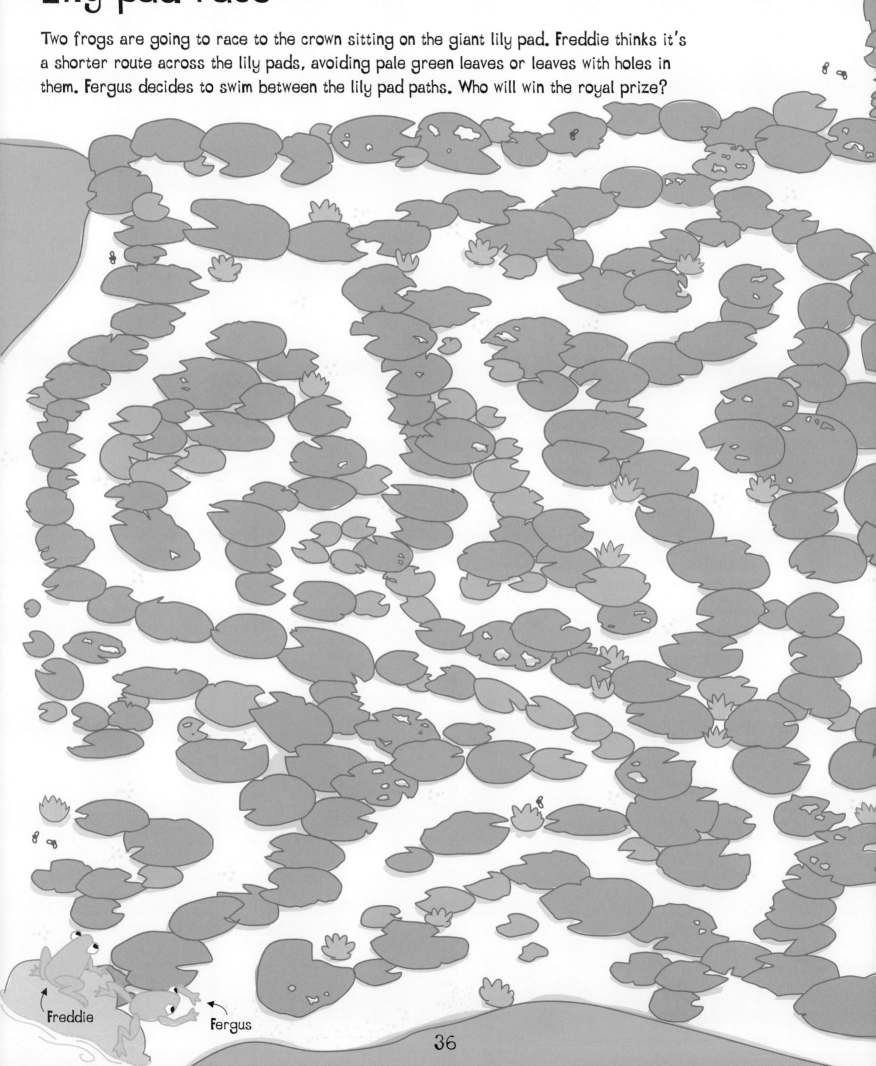

Freddie

Fergus

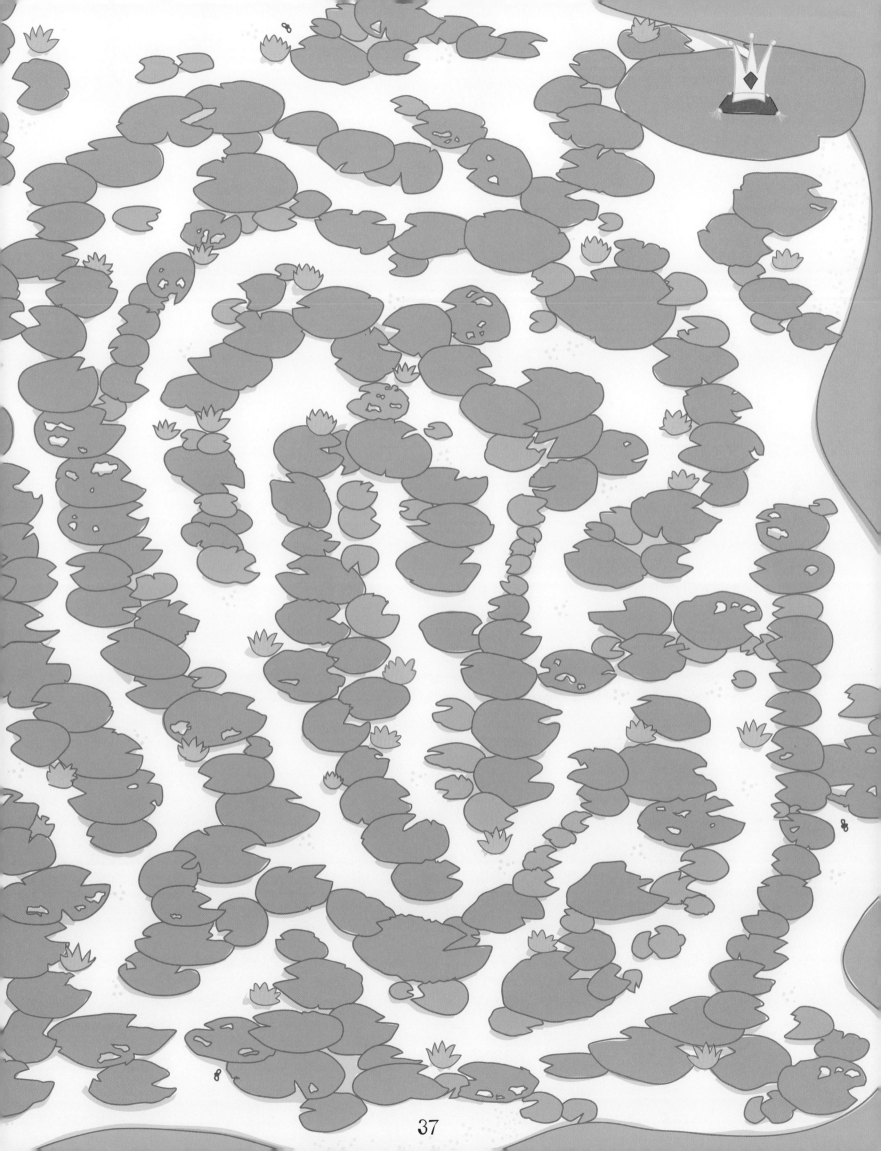

Desert disaster

Oh no! This jeep is lost in the desert. Which track should it take to reach the cooling pool at the oasis as quickly as possible? It can't drive over snakes.

Oasis

Busy bus

Which is the best route for the bus to drive to the bus station?
It must avoid dead-ends and red no-entry signs.

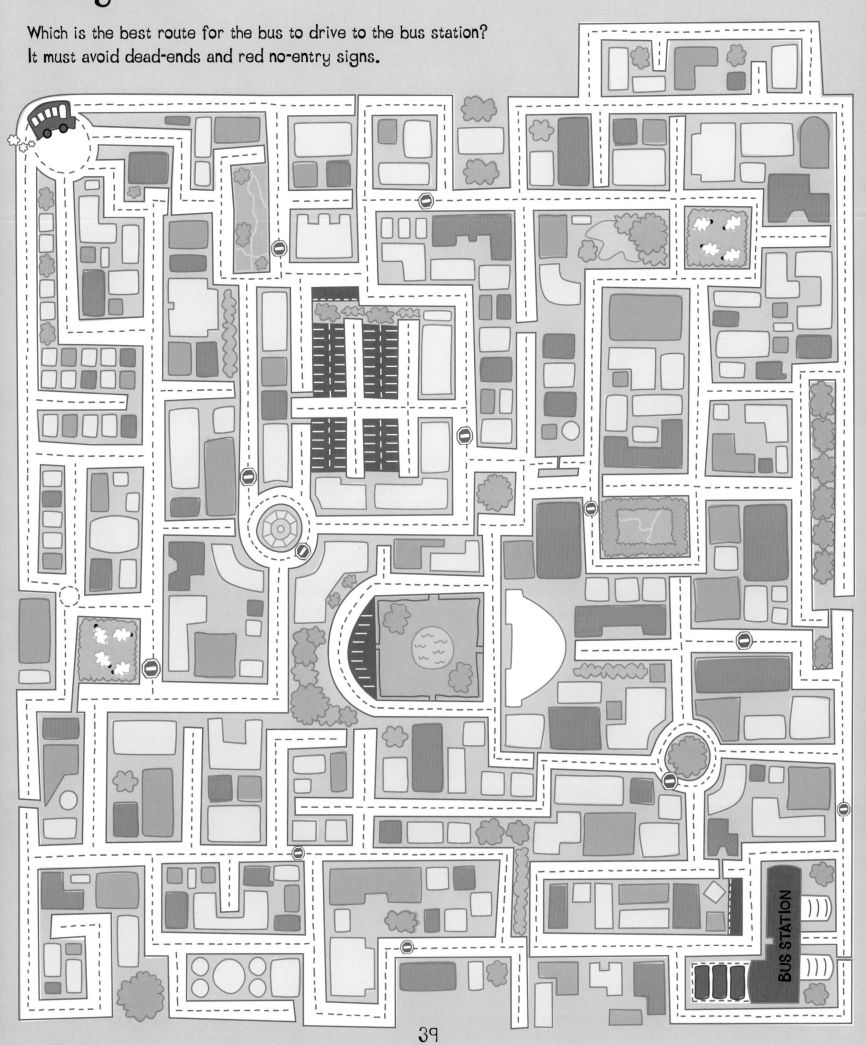

BUS STATION

39

Monkey puzzle

Help the little monkey find its friend.
It can scamper along any jungly vines, but
stepping on a snake would be a big mistake.

Little
monkey

Little
monkey's
friend

Hedgehog hurry

See if you can show the hedgehog family the way to the leaf pile so they can snuggle up warmly for winter.

Route race

The car that crosses over (but not under) the most bridges will reach the railway bridge first. Which car will it be?

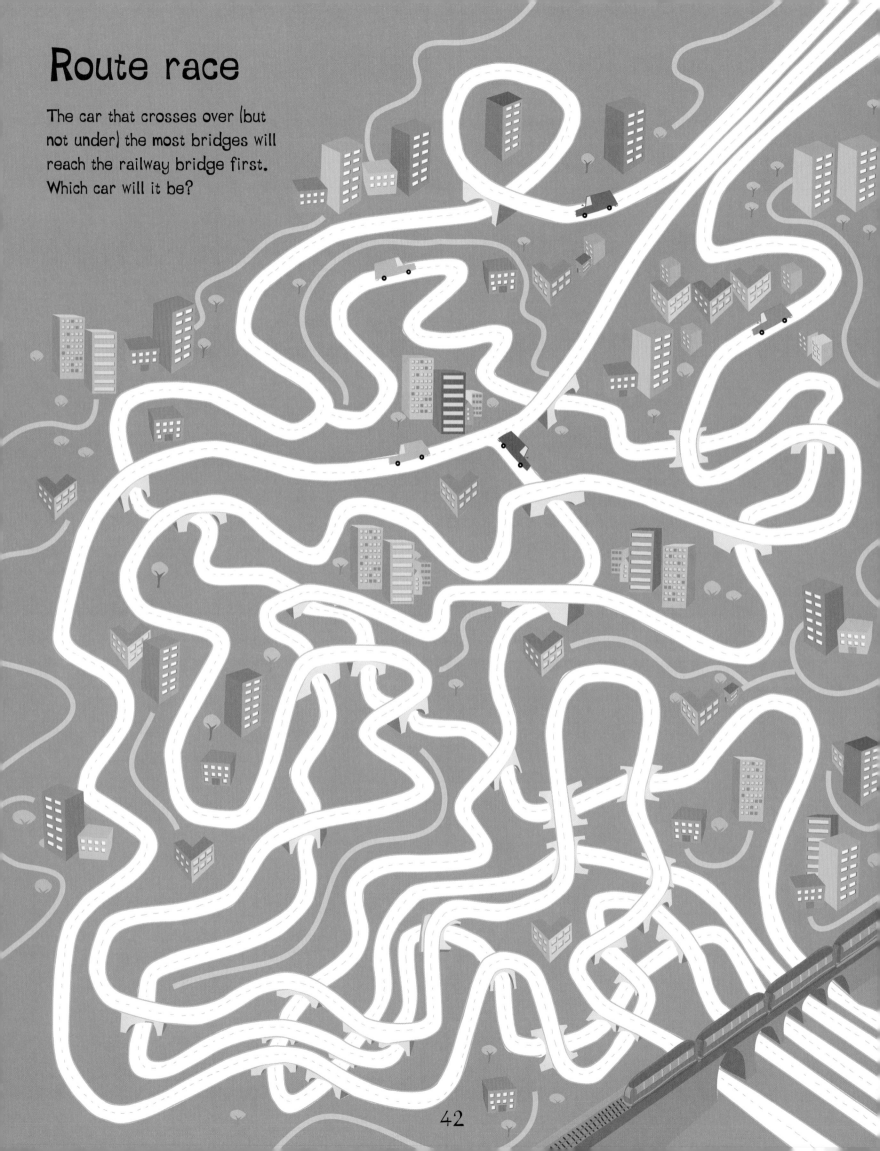

42

Super slalom

Help the skier complete his time trial by following the route that passes the green, orange and red flags but avoids the purple and blue flags.

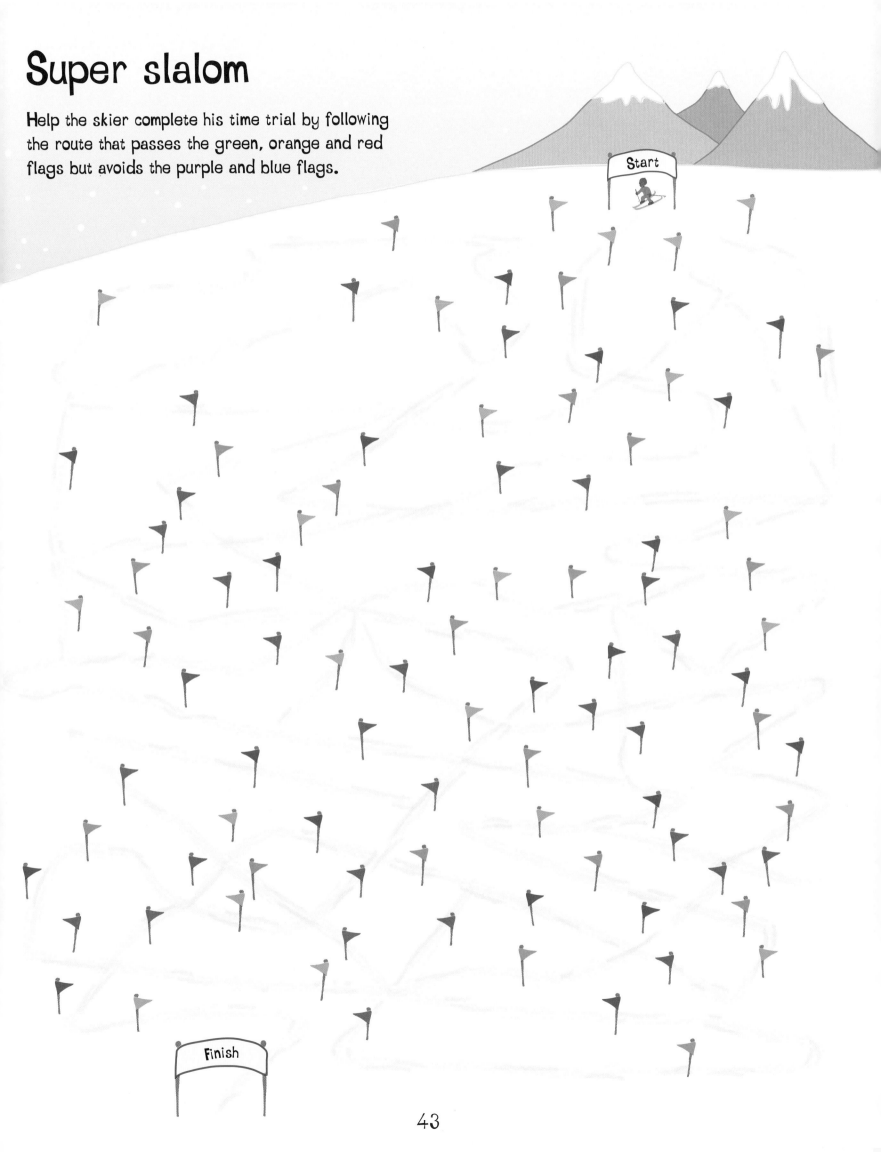

43

Apple maze

There's not much of this apple left to munch, but there are still some tasty seeds in the core. Which tunnels should Colin and Caspar take to reach them and who will win the race?

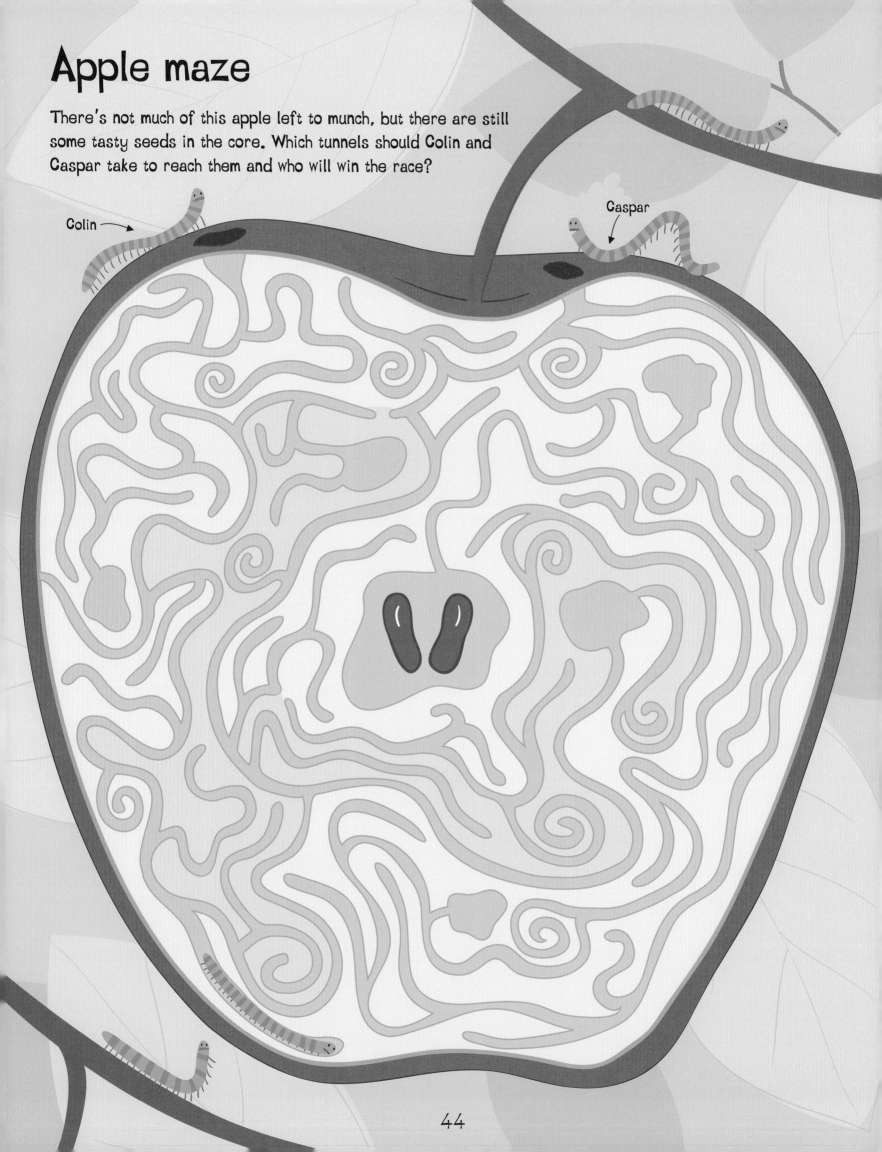

Colin

Caspar

Construction chaos

Find a way for Brian to reach the cab of the crane. He can swing around upright scaffolding poles, but can't get past brick walls or "Do not enter" signs, and he can only go up and down the scaffolding with a ladder.

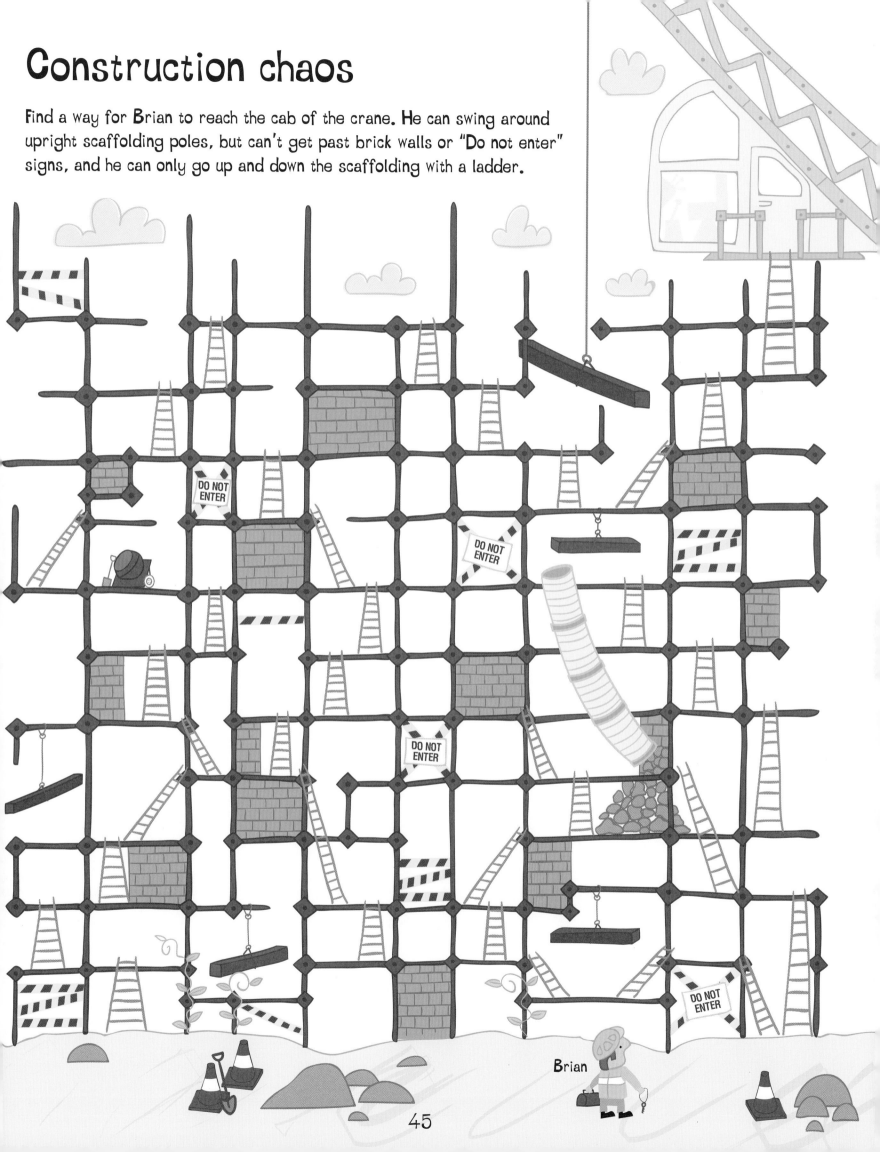

Peaks and valleys

Help the tourists wind their way between the mountain peaks to the Ramblers' Retreat at the top.

Start here

Lady Mary's gardens

Enter Lady Mary's gardens through the iron gate and find your way to the central fountain to feed the hungry fish. Please remember to keep off the grass.

Fish Pond

Plumbing puzzle

Which pipe will carry water
uninterrupted to the bathtub?
(The water can flow in
any direction as long as
its path is not blocked.)

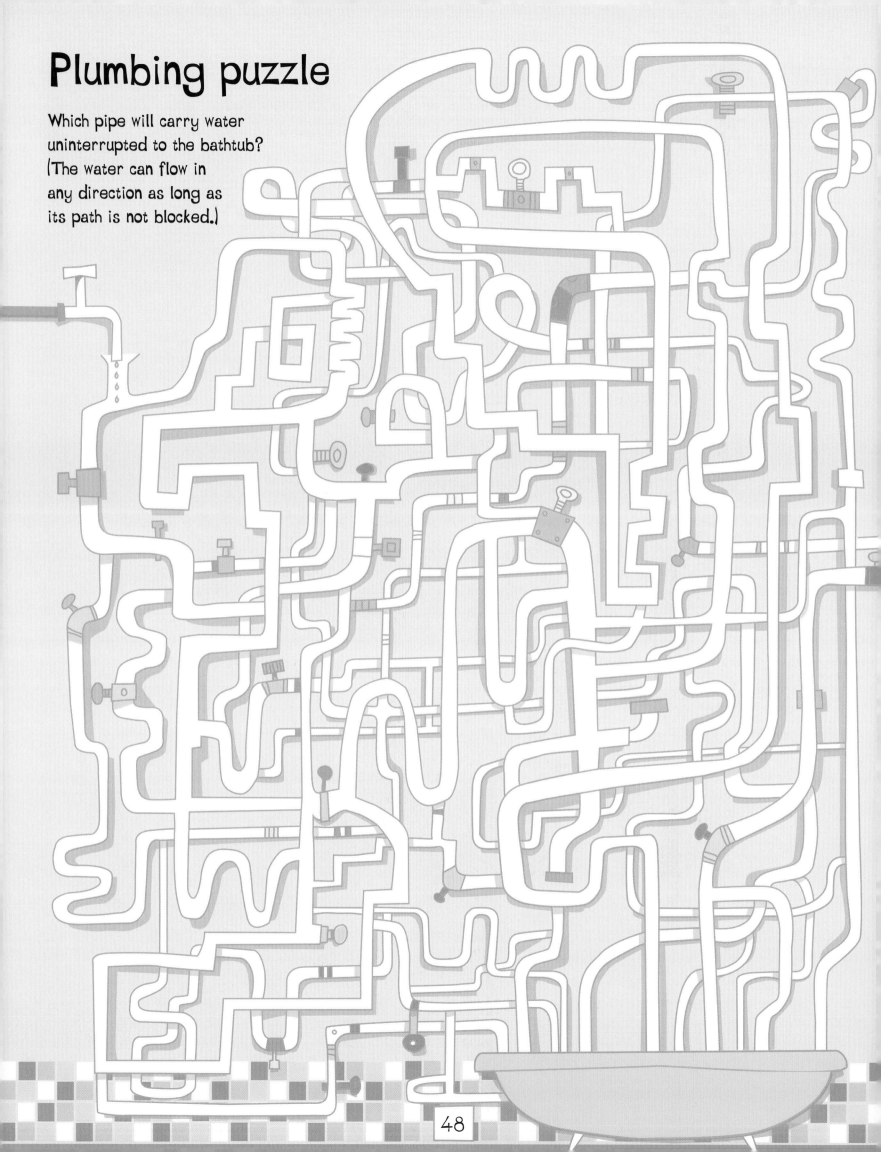

Apple orchard

Help the duck gather exactly six fallen apples on her way home. She can't take the same path twice or meet a hungry fox.

Nuts and bolts

Starting at the wrench, see if you can find a way to move around the machine to tighten every nut. You can't travel along any path more than once.

Nuts look like this.

Start here

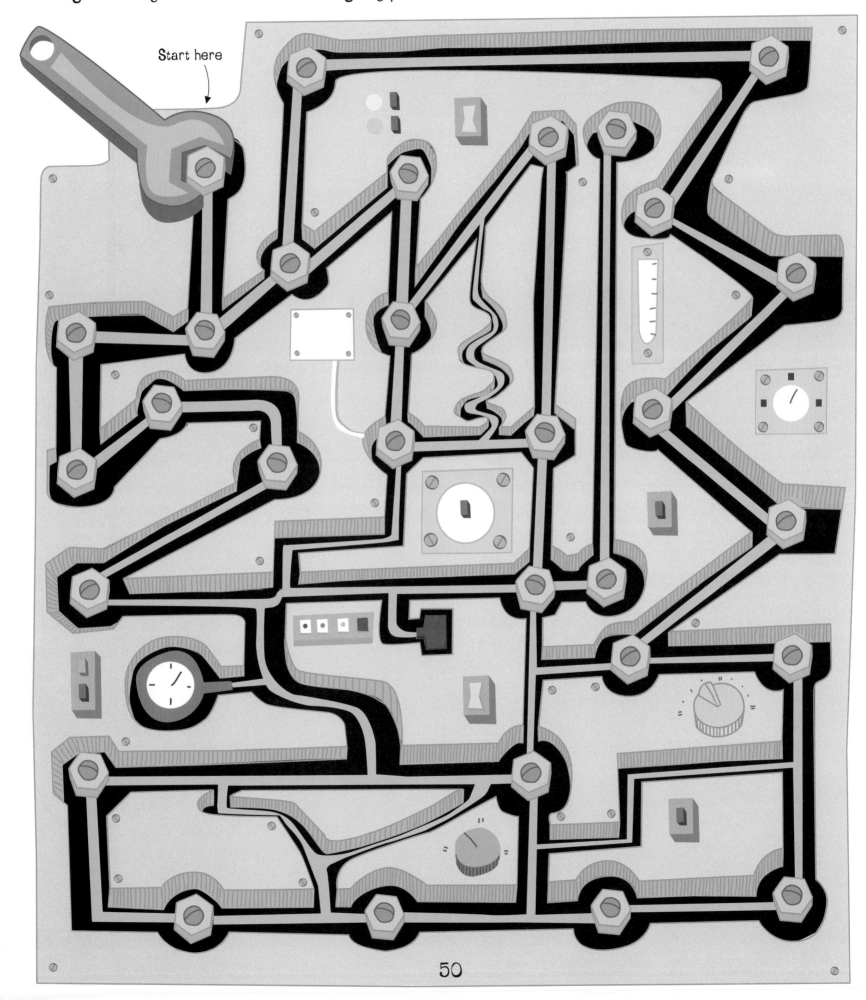

Circuit search

Help Robbie the robot find his way through the circuit maze to Rodney.
He can only change direction where there is a dot.

Rodney

Robbie

Mysterious mansion

Help! How can Spike get out of this spooky house? Starting in the attic, he must use every staircase or ladder once only. He must creep through every room but he may only go once through any doorway. Can he escape before he loses his nerve?

Spike

Sticky spider's web

Quick! See if you can weave your way between the sticky threads to save the frantic flies before the spider reaches them.

Start here

Runaway rollercoaster

Which route will lead the runaway rollercoaster safely to the end of the ride?

Start here

Tickets

End here

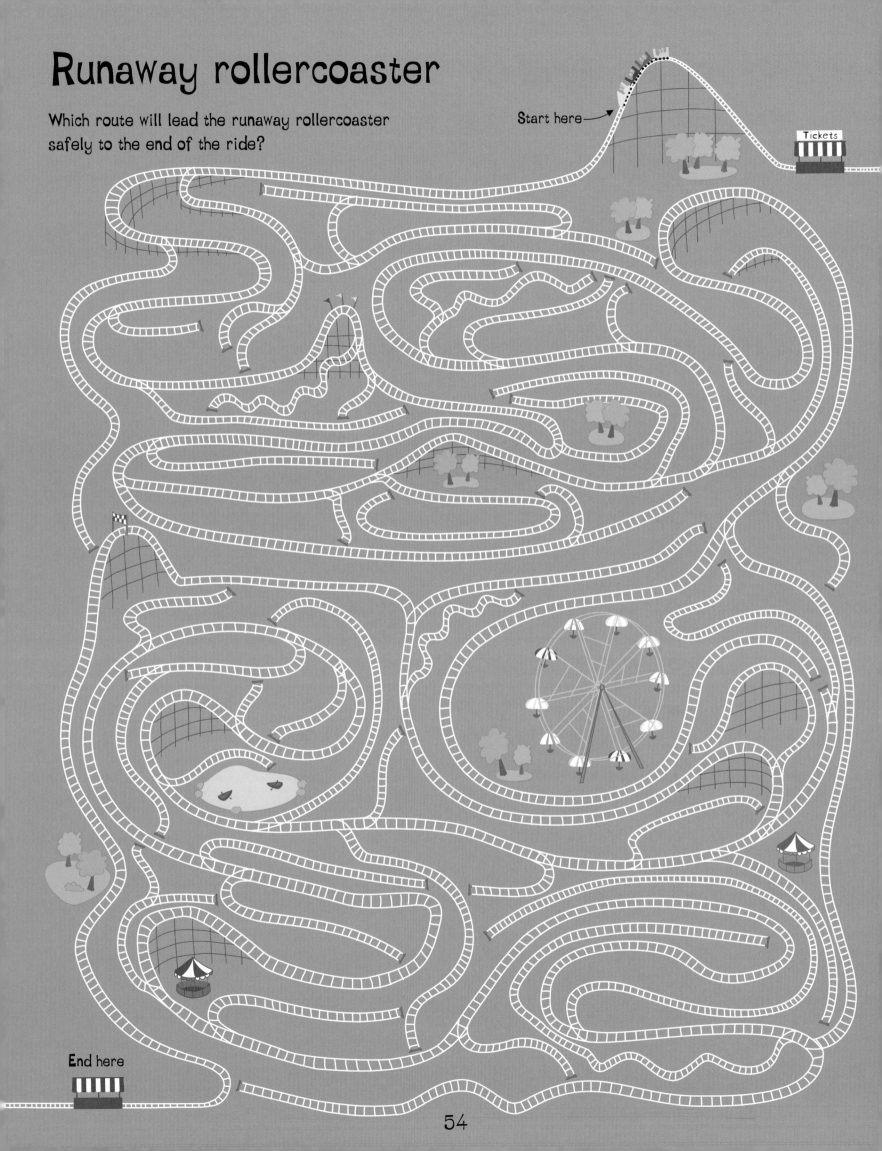

Coconuts ahoy!

The sailor needs to collect a coconut a day for a week-long voyage. Help him find a route across the ladders where every other tree he reaches has a coconut, so he can pick seven coconuts by the time he gets back to his boat. He can use each ladder only once.

End here

Start here

Puzzle pyramid

Starting at the bottom of the pyramid, can you find your way through the maze of passages to the pharaoh's tomb at the top? (Luckily, you have brought climbing equipment with you.)

Start here

Sheep search

Sheppie the sheepdog has lost his sheep. Which path should he take between the stone walls to find them?

Buzzing bees

Can you help these little bees through the honeycomb maze to visit their queen?
They can fit through any spaces in the white waxy walls.

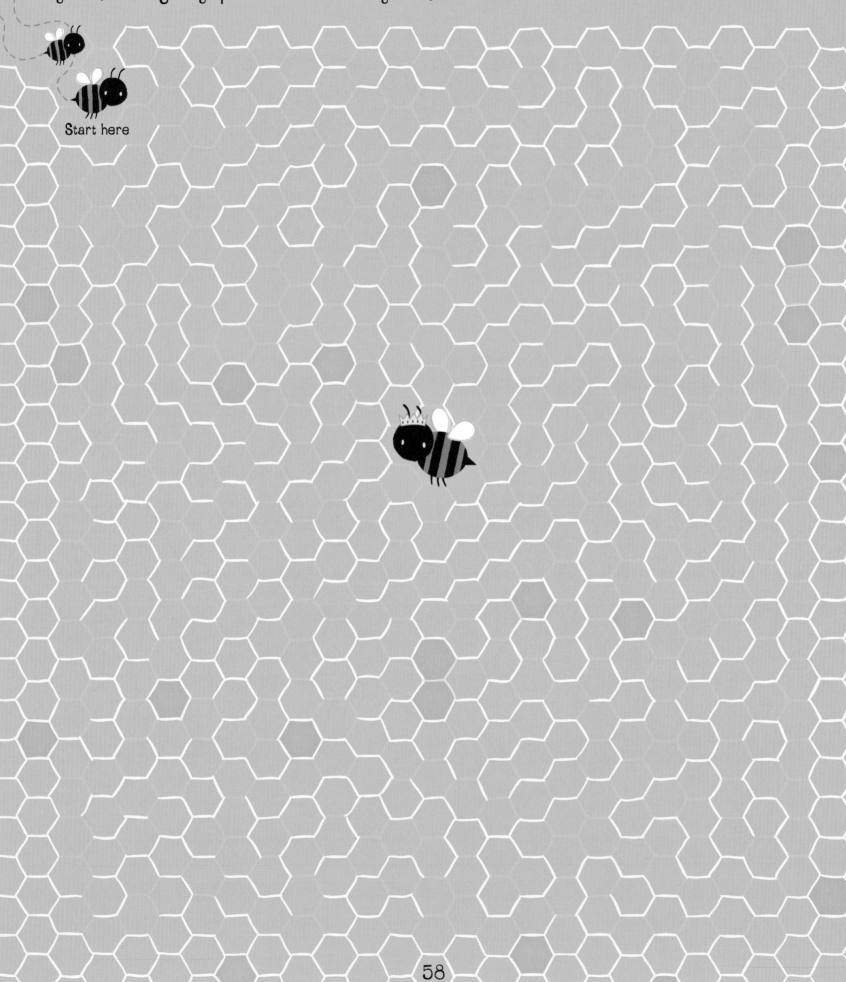

Start here

Monster messengers

These monsters "talk" to each other by touching arms.
Which way will the message travel from the orange
monster at the edge to its friend in the middle?

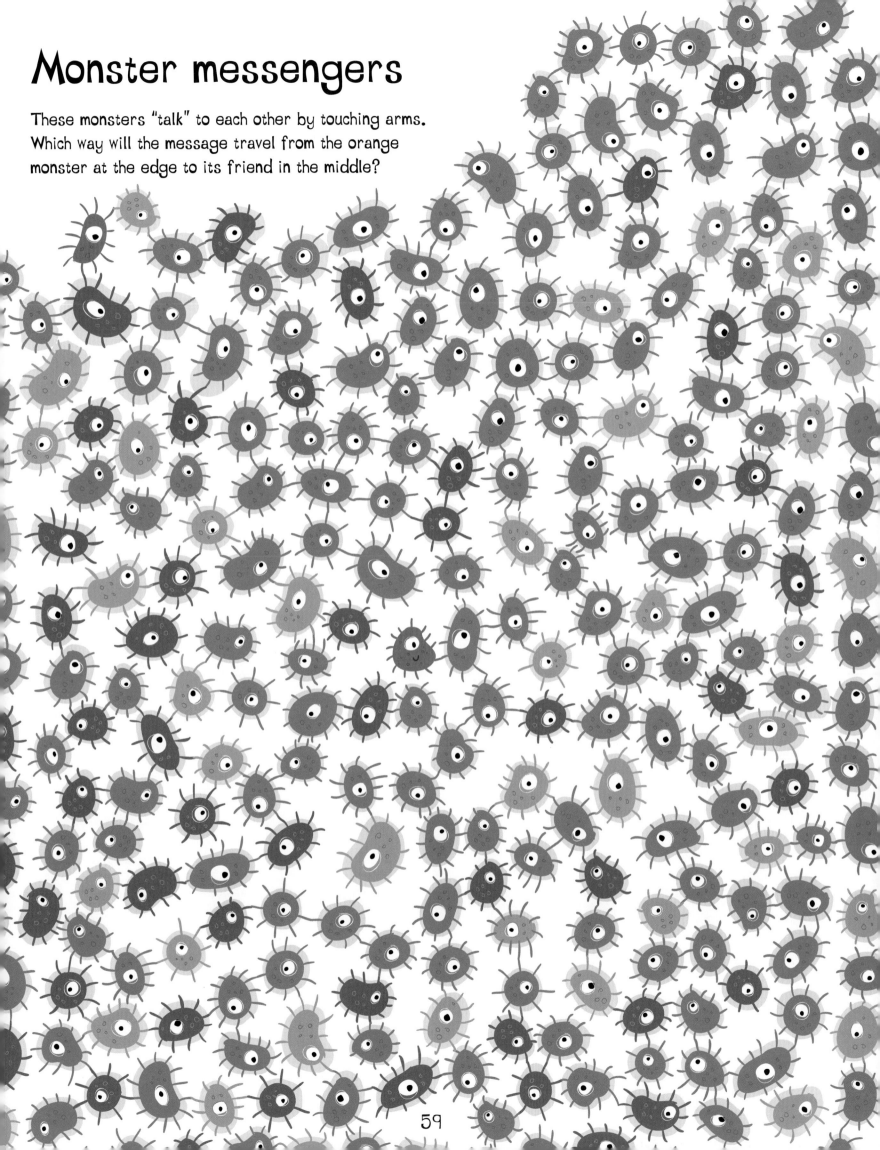

Gold rush

The gold cart has rolled all the way down from the top of the mountain. Can you help the miner find a safe route down to fetch it? He can't step on or over cracks and must avoid broken ladders and bridges.

He will have to walk around cracks.

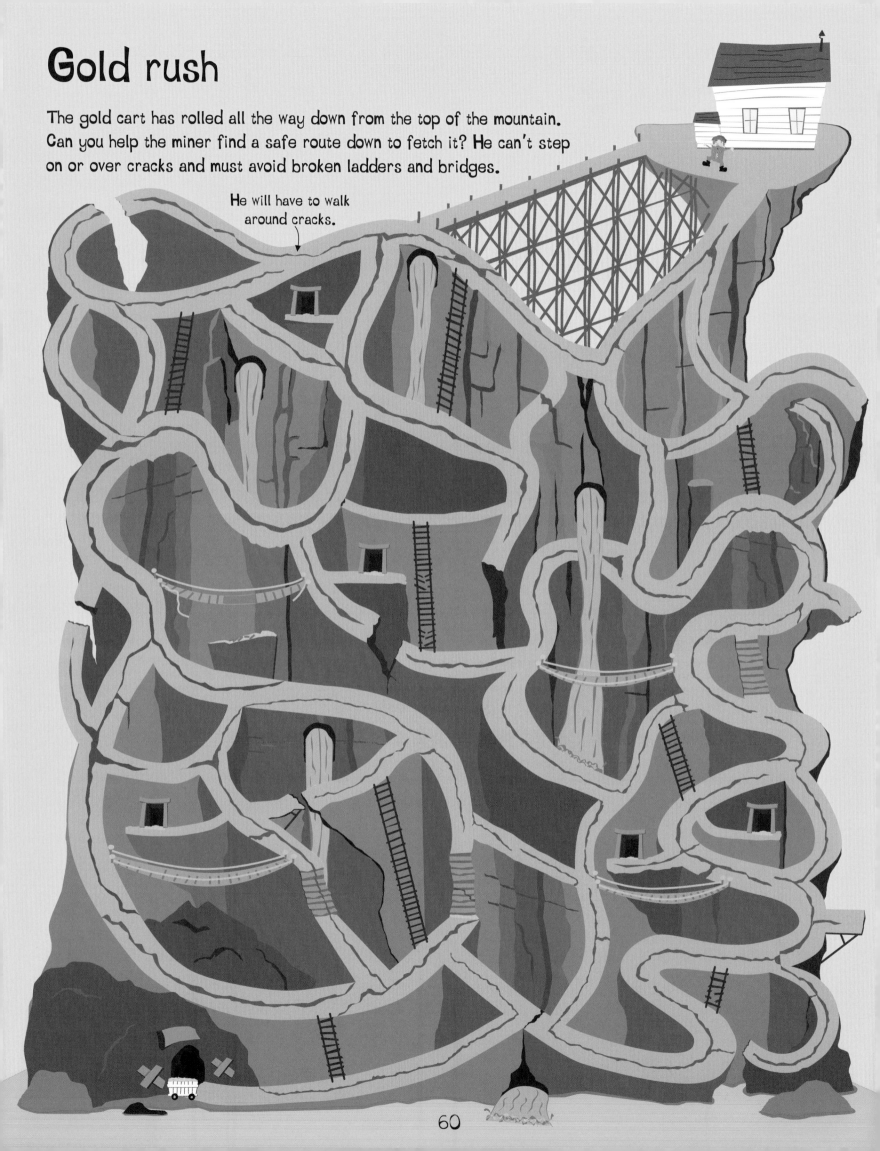

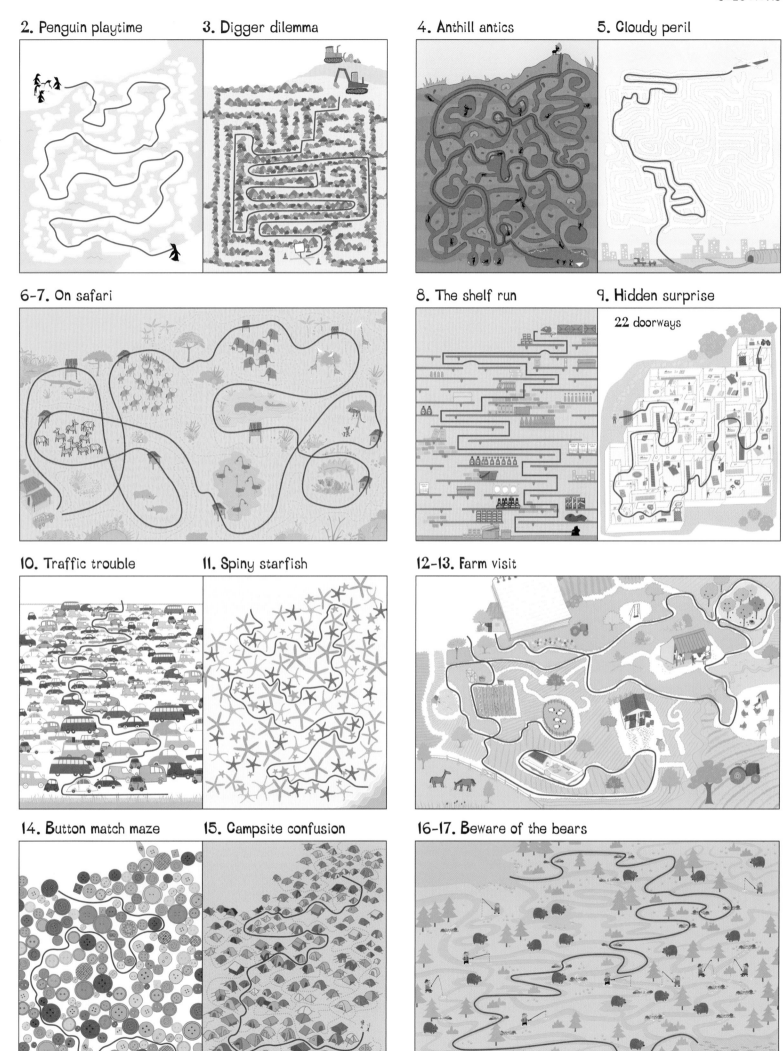

2. Penguin playtime

3. Digger dilemma

4. Anthill antics

5. Cloudy peril

6-7. On safari

8. The shelf run

9. Hidden surprise

22 doorways

10. Traffic trouble

11. Spiny starfish

12-13. Farm visit

14. Button match maze

15. Campsite confusion

16-17. Beware of the bears

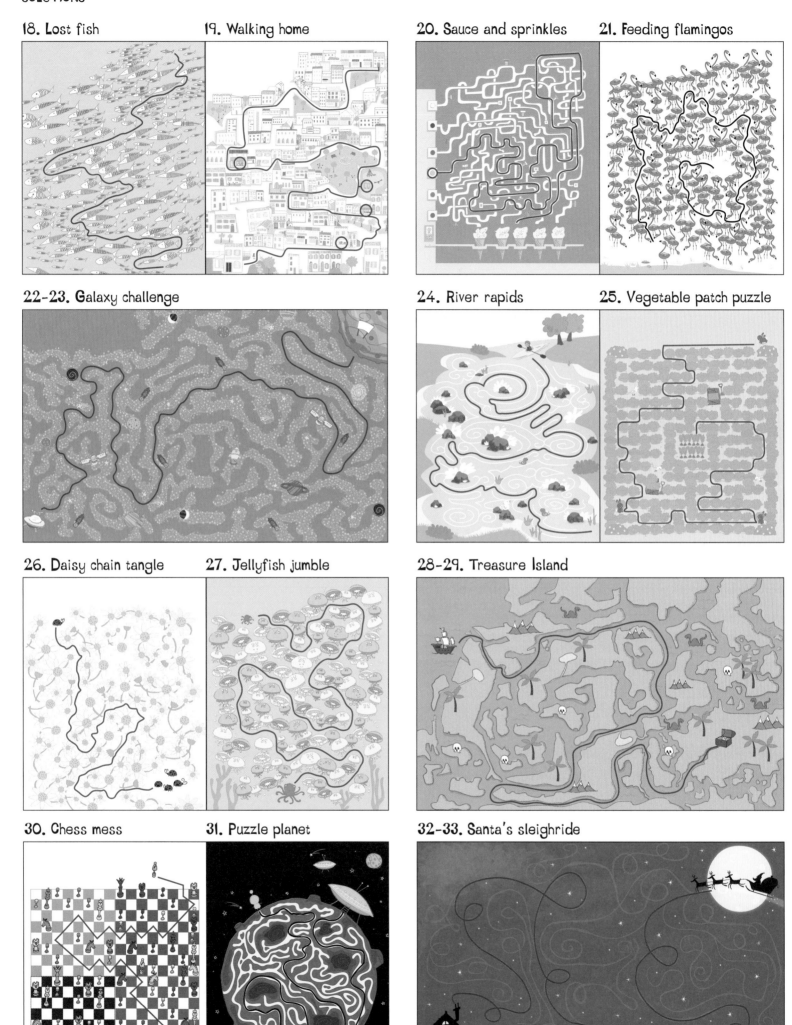

18. Lost fish

19. Walking home

20. Sauce and sprinkles

21. Feeding flamingos

22-23. Galaxy challenge

24. River rapids

25. Vegetable patch puzzle

26. Daisy chain tangle

27. Jellyfish jumble

28-29. Treasure Island

30. Chess mess

31. Puzzle planet

32-33. Santa's sleighride

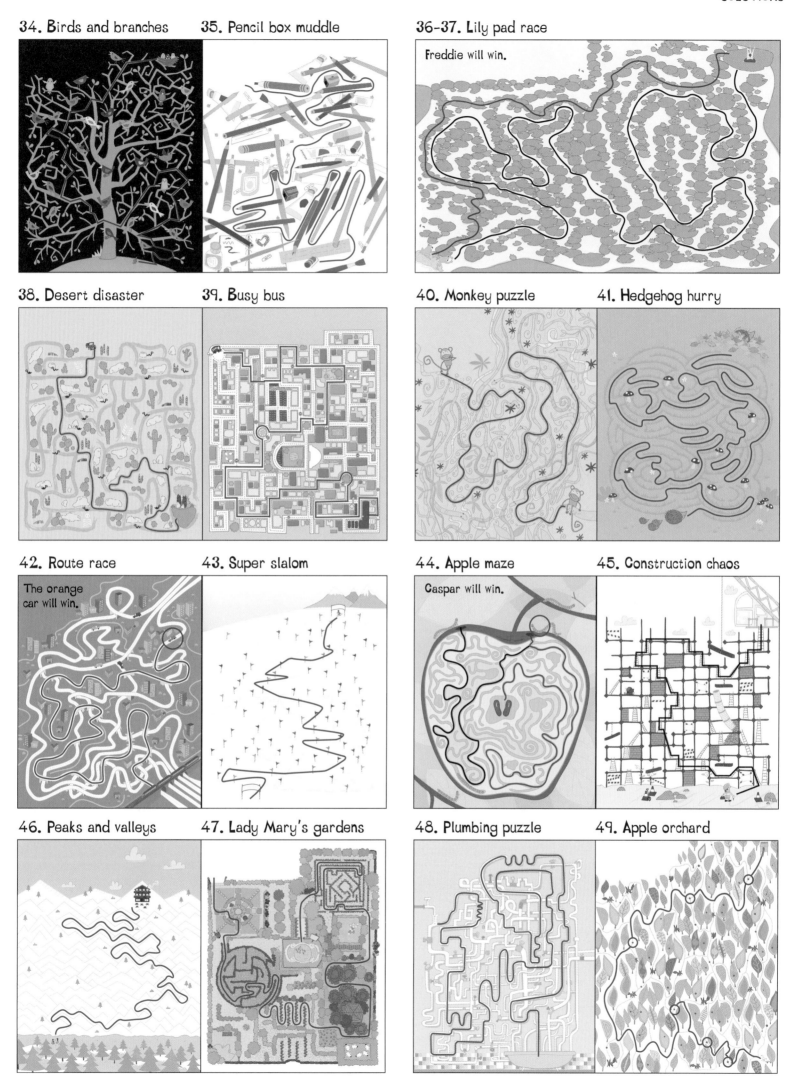

34. Birds and branches

35. Pencil box muddle

36-37. Lily pad race

Freddie will win.

38. Desert disaster

39. Busy bus

40. Monkey puzzle

41. Hedgehog hurry

42. Route race

The orange car will win.

43. Super slalom

44. Apple maze

Caspar will win.

45. Construction chaos

46. Peaks and valleys

47. Lady Mary's gardens

48. Plumbing puzzle

49. Apple orchard

50. Nuts and bolts
51. Circuit search
52. Mysterious mansion
53. Sticky spider's web

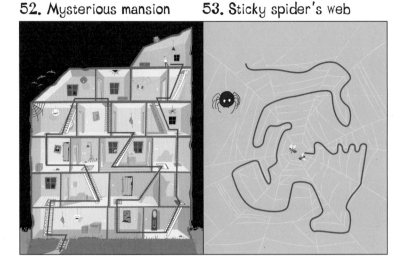

54. Runaway rollercoaster
55. Coconuts ahoy!
56. Puzzle pyramid
57. Sheep search

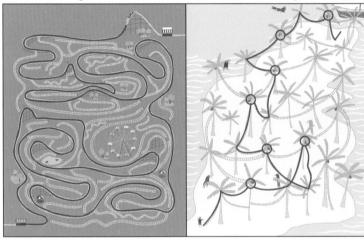

58. Buzzing bees
59. Monster messengers
60. Gold rush

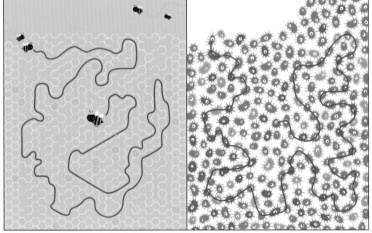
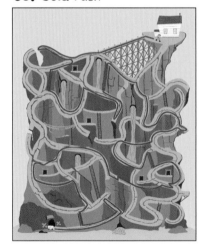

Acknowledgements

Additional designs by
Laura Hammonds, Marc Maynard and Keith Furnival

With thanks to our maze testers:
Zachary Boachie-Barrance, Janey Harold, Faye Jones, Jack Middleton